# the incense(d) heart

not another poetry collection

*indeed, another poetry collection*

**Maha Zimmo**

*Also by Maha Zimmo*

rose-water syrup

*a dedication –*


*for them, who said i do not like poetry*
*for them, who said i do not understand poetry*
*so that you may know yourself*
*so that you may love yourself.*

a small charcoal-haired girl sits in an empty oyster shell.

she is wearing a blood-red dress
ornate slippers of sea and sand
roots
which she often refuses
to take off.

not reaching the marble floor,
she swings her feet
catching the wind
everything sing-songs *Salaam*
her mouth forms *hello*.

flattening the skirts of her dress
eyes wide
curious
watching her elders,
a photograph yellow, fading.

there is an antique mirror
pearl inlaid
to her left.
hopeful,
the mirror pulls at her rose-on-olive cheeks
to keep her
as company
where all that is reflected –
present, self.

the girl turns from the mirror.

surrounded by night sky, star-full

she throws a tiny net into the darkness.

she will catch rose-water stars
write structure
to honour her ancestors.

- step into past to form our present

occupied and colonized
the song of my heart-country.

it is
that gentle echo of bell
the note of her charm(ed) bracelet
a moving Brown hand

to rearrange
reimagine
rearticulate
already perfect rose-water skin
beneath veils of silk
tau(gh)t
that *as is*
is too full.


- the shrinking | for the comfort of White gaze

curiosity piqued
inside the blood rush
a mouth hot,
crimson,
i run my tongue across swollen lips
where he has not touched me
yet.

- anticipation

at the edge of a hidden dip
he runs his eyes across the valley
measuring the distance between ridges
required
to swim across rose-water oceans.

his thumb
kisses the hollow
at the base of this neck
before his mouth
draws the map of my body.

- cartographer

you are used to seeing People of Colour
ask your permission to validation.

bleed apologies for behaviours of others
all-the-same-shade-to-you Others.

you are used to seeing People of Colour
fade into your history
but brighten your narrative
seeing yourselves
while wearing your eyes
and never seeing themselves
eye-to-eye
toe-to-toe
but doubtless taller.

- this is why you don't like me | you need a new prescription

she is flowed between his fingers
run over his tongue
bitten at his teeth
thrown into heat
gently
turned over and around for inspection.

his hands, pressure exerted the perfect calibration
bottom lip moist
soft, holds and keeps her rhythmic landings.

she is his extension, outside
he becomes her expansion, inside.

ending near
he is faster to come for her
shorter, more concentrated breaths
frow burrowed, eyes shut, chest constricted
pause
exhale
into calmed nerves.

- cigarette

1.  Skin, molasses and honey.
2.  Veins, passion-full.
3.  Almond eyes, witness.
4.  Dusted brows, Allah-kissed.
5.  Fig-swelled tongues, machetes.

- Home | Where We Were

1. bleached skin.
2. alcohol veins.
3. eyes turned.
4. facing West.
5. crisped bacon.

- immigrant | where we are

your mouth parted in sleep
i leaned over
and rested a prayer there.

- temple is rarely a building

i stare
slip a hand across my neck
rest on
heartbeat, wild
rage-full
*breathe*, i remind myself.

*but unity*
they wrote.

all bodies, not White
are under threat
historically, and at present
future too, if we do not burn it all
use as kindling this moment
to come from ashes
anew
divorced. apart. shattered. and splintered
from this very privilege of your
*but unity*
peace-keeping only, and for none other
than you
and all bedfellows
moral acrobats
ensuring your comfort
sat on cushions
atop the lungs of those for whom
you declared
a black square.

- the performative peep show

*do you let men touch you*
*it is the road to Hell.*

my body freezes beneath his
legs pinned by their voices

i have stopped breathing

filled with sickness
i am taught that my belly,
like the earth, my core a liquid heat,
this thirst
to be loved
skin's hunger
to be held
are the diseases
that will turn Him from me.

i split in half
seeking salvation -

my body is a disease
my skin is filthy.

my heart is pure
my soul is flawless.

this civil war
is the reason
my body is drawn to one man
while my heart, it loves another.

this civil war
it is (is it?) the very reason
i cannot marry the man i bed
and cannot bed the man i marry.

*love is not haraam*, i remind myself
*but i will corrupt a wedding dress, pollute it with grime, i*
respond.

- paradise lost | maladjusted communion

he kissed like Times New Roman.


you,
like hand-written letters
swelled by humidity
at the tip of fingers stained by honey & cinnamon trees.

- the easy choice to make

the bottom
red colours the curve
beneath your brow
carefully placing itself
cushions-full
to rest in the space where you taste
like peace.

- this mouth

you were so anxious
to show
that the colour of your blood is like theirs –

irrigated your mouth with alcohol
kept lovers without mercy (between you)
raised children on shame
faces turned from Him
forgetting the softness.

i found you
fragmented
neither with me, nor there
folded your hand into mine
led you to His shores.

i bathed you in rose-water syrup
partook of it from your mouth
we drank at temple
to seek forgiveness
always His
forgetting our own.

gently here
your eyes sprang fresh water
while salt-water
pulled your feet to her ocean floor
roots, she revealed
reminding you of
your beauty.

- Muslim rite(s) | a baptism

trusting
that people will do the wrong thing
for all of the right reasons.

- salvation | how to keep the softness i

my tongue
is still at war
between who I am
and the i that makes
White people comfortable.

these lacerating poems
stuck inside my gut
breathe deepest
and land heaviest
at the feet of White people
when
i
am too scared
to fight this battle
but
I
swell my voice
though tremble still.

- a multitude of civil wars

my skin carries history
the stories of men
before you

i wonder if
you read their secrets
of braille.

- tactile interference

he entered through the wrong door
(surprising me again)

with a single paper in hand
he nicked my arm,
moved back into shadow.

i put the cut to my mouth
waited for the bleeding to stop
(like all other times).

except that day
my body burned
and tasted like suns setting.

- when i bled out (to my own surprise) | watch out equally for
the paper-cuts as the machete'd gashes

you have the freedom
to close your chest
regarding the pain of other.

you are free
to mock silence
when turning from
the pain of other.

it is your god(s)-given right
to choose apathy,
who cares about
the pain of other.

but do not

saucer your eyes
when we turn our backs
(shred your suddenly displaced
tongues, dancing
to our amusement)
while you
blood-gurgle
*'please choose different
than me.'*

- hypocrites

she falls back into his pillows
soft, used clouds
suffocating in cloth skins.

matching his,
ink black, her hair
it catches
she runs her fingers
to unlock traps.

her hand
always memory in her skin
a mind of its own
a déjà vu
finds the hair with her third eye
intuitive.

she holds the hair to her face.

"did you recently have a blonde in this bed?"

(shrugs)
"of course not."

- out of body experience

*it is in your self-interest*
*to find a way to be understanding.*

but

there are days
when it is impossible to exercise. lean into. engage. extend to
others
honestly. and with selflessness
understanding.

days
when my back curves
to protect this mutilated chest
bleeding heart.

days
when my feet are paralyzed
blisters from all the walking. beating around. running to meet
you half-way
up the very hill
your ancestors built
to your ease
and my exclusion.

days
when my throat is raw
from the talking. explaining. praying
you understand
the trauma
at the hands of. by too many of them
others.

days
when i am sorrow-full
when the trauma is so deep. and thick. and lush
that i would rather sink in. and look in. and care in
than exercise anything
toward this outside
most definitely not
understanding
toward an other.

- i do not owe you a conversation

single women, divorced women,
candy beneath split tongues
inside infested mouths
putrefied tissue
and tongue.

my culture, but not my deen,
makes women
consumable
fodder for the mouths

of others -
who have men in their homes
castrated.

of others –
who sneer behind yellowed hands
stretched beneath
designer names covering insides
rotten
mouths filled with larva
laid by ego
hatched by insecurity
attracted to your words
foul.

Muhammad said
all would be safe across lands alone
within his kingdom;
only this today-kingdom
mocks the safe-keeping he promised
this today-kingdom
maggot ravaged
gluttonous,

gorging on the skins pulled across our backs,
this today-kingdom
what a shameful kingdom
see-through
to everyone but itself.

- heart disease of this unGodly kingdom

be careful what you look for
in case
you see what isn't there
just to prove you were right
to look for it in the first place.

because always
it is better
that your trust is shattered
than
your suspicions
proven false.

- how to keep the softness ii

i offered my heart, carefully seasoned
years-long marinated.

i did not know
when he took it into his hands
its metal
would eventually flood my mouth.

- aftertaste

requiring neither validation, nor permission
the most beautiful outfit in the room
is shaded secure, and confident
with shoes coloured humility, and always learning.

- burn your magazines | us, beautiful ghouls

to my service
how may i siphon her natural resources
while expending the least amount of energy?

- the male gaze, translated

my hand in his
when the man approached and asked
*can you help me*
*anything will help.*

my hand in his
when he chuckled and said
*only if you have change for a hundred.*

my hand in his
suddenly wet-slippery-unholdable his
pulled away and took out all she had
offered with shame and apology
and never made her way back to
my hand in his
ever again.

- some endings sing right

sunday(s)
sitting next to you
when i saw that
i
had not laid eyes on you
in years.

- conceit of the farsighted

if he could not provide the richness of love
i would erase his wealth of coins.

this is how i punished my father.

i had not realized that
where he could not speak it
he burned it into every penny.

- 'i love you' | different love languages

once

a strange man
pulled my ponytail.

a strange man
ran his hands through my hair.

a strange man
reached between my legs and grabbed my gut.

a strange man
felt between his legs and cupped his brain.

a strange man
pulled down his pants to fuck the wind.

a strange man
pulled down his shorts to stroke his ego.

a strange man
helped himself to my breast.

a strange man
jerked himself into his other hand.

eight
i can recount without effort.

no women. not one.

but please
keep hashtagging yourself out of this equation.

- #notallmen

smiling

i slid your razor across my right eye
and then across my left
the blood pooled, guiding my hand
to where i cut and removed my tongue
which i placed gently on my bedside table.
exchanging the razor for a needle
which i pushed through
first my left ear
and then my right.

ending,
you walked over
draped your vestment over my heart.

- because this was the only way i could lie with you

at eleven,

i feel an echo in my chest.

i count backwards from ten.

ten times
since i pressed six
to open the door
for others.

ten times
your presence was still listed
visible. tangible. quantifiable
proof
that you were once. with me.

- missing evidence

you have experienced
the women
arid for your attention
the good. the bad. mostly ugly
attention
water, poured into glass
with jagged edges
fine shards

puncturing and sliding into nubile flesh

openings blood-dripping

water now rose-coloured
consumed a sacrament
praying. waiting. excusing
at the altar of
you.

until she
who refuses the bloodletting. and self-sacrifice
in your name. for your side-gaze. slippery words,
the good. the bad. mostly ugly
attention.

woman
whose altar is
herself.

- dawn

crusading fingers
you glide in
to softness
a body
already built in sand
cleansed by salt-water seas
skin of honey
crown of waves.

crusading fingers, impressions leaving
my body
now reorganized between your hands,
i am suddenly a chalice,
your hands declare as new existing land
already home to one heart
to my body's one wall
the only one i cannot rebuild
which you claim alone for yourself.

- colonizer's hym(e)n

tears in my palms like raindrops
the monsoon is unrelenting
i am a beggar.

prayers,
offerings of and by my self
braided meticulously
into one sheet of terror with
*fear of receiving love*
*fear of abandonment.*

their hands sandpapered to increase friction
stronger as they undo themselves from my gut
one by one climbing the cage
forced to come up into my mouth
where i must recognize them
before they hook into the softness of ivory
forceful with their display of strength
falling from this mouth into my palms
where i may wrap and place them
wet with blood
gently at the corner of my prayer rug.

- what i want deepest is that which terrifies me most

to watch
the sun light her match
to kiss
the moon wet with rose-water syrup
from inside the right arms.

- prayer | الدعاء

100 million
kidnapped
from their mother(land)
broken
tongues cut
into enslavement.

25 million
stood
to walk 'freedom'.

still all
fight for equity
recognition
they are
the reason
America's soil
is so rich.

- this on-going genocide

which do you care for more
conformity
or
humanity?

it cannot be both.

- community care | on why i have never loved a conformist

he advances on her
intentional
sticky fingers catch beneath her breast
snapping ribs
wet mouth wraps around the soft bone
siphoning mineral deposits,
bloodied nipple
as cherry on top.

all the while
glamour words glide across his forked tongue:
*empowerment. equity. choice.*

'ripcord from patriarchy'.

- beware the new misogyny

who has taught you
that your need for love
ought to make of you
easy prey?

for those of us made to feel unloved.
for those among us made to feel less. beneath. incomplete.

remember,
they fear outside what they lack inside.

you
everything
*you are whole.*

you
the very complexity
of what they fear
what they lack
what they do not wish to face
*you are abundant.*

you
*you are exquisite*
and they know.

- a love letter

women are socialized to find our value in the gaze of men.

a not-so-gentle reminder –

your value has never
not once
has it hinged on how any man has viewed you.

your value has never been
nor will it ever be
contingent on the presence of any man in your life.

your value is.

your
value
*Is*.

by your presence
and kindness toward others,
your value *Is*.

- Post Script to a love letter

eternal,
you are cared for
being guided through
every gracious happiness
articulate confusion
and blistering heart-pain.

intuitions
gut feelings
dreams
among the different languages
of One voice.

open your chest
to this galaxy of care
an oasis among the parched tongues
and withered actions
of others.

- multilingual refuge

kindness. integrity. honesty.
behaviours distorted
*fake news.*

people
with hearts in rigor mortis, faces in sand dunes
are left
to those among us
(softened by the beatings
our smiles stretched and pinned wide)
believers in good
believers in character
moral compass pointing Love.

people forced
to carry
their balance
because
because
*because*
if we do not
find this strength
we will be buried
beneath the weight of them
moral compass pointing Hate.

- keeping others to keep ourselves

be grateful
for every teacher
even when
you want to bloody knuckles
against syllabus.

- knowledge

footsteps like rose-petals
you stepped out from shadow
smiled
and i saw moonlight
festival of lights
all lanterns' glow moisten your hair.

you rise above me
counterfeit,
your tongue blushed, before my mouth
your body stuttered, between my hands.

eyes shut, ignoring shadow
pretending it shade
i lived in the light of your fastened smile
but
i believe the arteries
across my palms (k)new.

in wonder, i slowly peeled the smallest whisper
from the roads lining my hand.
hopeful then, slowly then, thumb as pen
i wrote my curiosity across your mouth,
hot.

your body, frozen
evaporated the heat of my question
pushing us into a wide fog
behind which you conjured
then slid
through a trap door.

- the (missing) magician

to build a home for him

in this softness
i did turn an eye blind
refused to believe
even as i watched him
tuck into it,
enthusiastically
*shuckin' and jivin',* he would say.

when he cannot exercise it
it extends to all matters –
substances
the bodies of others
and his tongue, he spins
a thousand tiny lacerations left.

untrustworthy without it
the very thing over which He asked us
to exercise control
of which he has none.

- impulse of the nafs/body-self

you are my favourite reason
to lose sleep.

- secrets i

chimes
danced on my wrist
rang at your ear
caught your hair
keeping you awake.

removed
quietly placed by your window
so you could rest without sound
your (newborn) head in the palm of my hand
fingers resting on your heart.

did you keep them
to hear my voice?
i wonder.

- curiosities

at daybreak,

i offered my love.

he took it
turned it upside down
moved it unnaturally sideways
threw it upwards into the clouds.

at twilight,
i watched him
catch my love
fold it into a small bulb
plant it gently into his lashes,
thickened with heaven's clouds
blinding the next woman to come,

at daybreak.

- con artist

you are choking
raging through salt-water.

your mind
fills with everything
through which
nothing
and too much
screams.

sadness lines your eyes
exhausted, shut tight
against the murkiness of deep blue
bruises
surfacing the misery of your pain.

my body you branded: life raft.

suffocating
my chest breaks
beneath the weight of you
the last straw your eyelashes
butterflies against my inflamed torso
but still
i place your head in my hands
send Quran through palms
to calm your mind
to slow your heart
to push you to shore
and lose myself.

- lost at sea

you appear
without invitation.
i write your face
like a small tremble
into
out of
into and out of
my incense(d) heart.

i pick you up, dress you
put on your glasses. dishevel your hair
(because this is how i liked you)
place you against an outdoor backdrop
decay colours leaves
there is a coffee bar to your right
haunted, without customers
to your immediate left, a table
missing a foot, it sags away from you.
i add a book in your hand
tattered, spine broken, pages missing
a pretty girl in your line of vision
she is nothing like me.

i write you into her love story
and drop my own heart
but not before i drive it into my throat
because i have no news of you
and this is the hardest news to ignore.

will i survive
all of my distortions
i wonder.


- smoke and mirrors | overactive imagination

"it is my most treasured book
battered and fragile
pages undone after too many readings.

keep it safely wrapped
inside its satin ribbon
so none of it is lost."

- the (unreturned) loan as metaphor

*all of my exes would get angry & upset*
said the man
who failed at maths.

- he, the (only) common denominator

you dressed your mouth in honey lemon
i fed on the sweet
until acid cut my voice.

you said
i will wash you in moonlight
so
i bathed in rays
until night sky turned to sharpest day
searing my skin.

*he left nothing*
*but pain*
*refusing this as his only offering*
*i chose instead to fall in love with it*
*and write him from my body.*

the smallest font
tightly wound
creating unique
individual
fingerprints.

every softness
of this body is still covered in you,
your fingerprint words.

this is how
i write you from my skin.

*he left nothing*
*i filled it with poetry.*

- one way my body gives me poetry

i would unlearn
all books
if
i could read
your skin
once more.

- library

clues left -

she builds
bouquets of local flowers
swells them with love
into small cups she arranges them.

clouds sewn, a quilt of darkness
she knits her way through alleys
bouquets as beacons
found the next morning
next to sleeping men.

- love gifts from the rose-water traveler

i wish
i were writing you love letters
instead.

- secrets ii

chemistry –
it is a story
written onto bodies
incised by fingernails
etched by urgent friction
for second. third. fourth time readings.

our chemistry –
it was not a story
worth
reading again.

- lessons from lover(s) after

i was a fever dream

earth in my gentleness
cosmos between us
home in my eyes.

i spoke with a new tongue
it was seamless rapids,
effervescence,
offered honey at your temple
warmth, tracing down your ribcage.

forehead to my feet,
my body, your temple.

- what you gave up

when a flame
burns paper
they become one,
but this, too, it is not love.

- union

if you had shown me
which parts of you are empty
i would have cut from me

to fill you.

- the thing(s) you had but did not deserve

all heart-pain,
found in the undoing
of one from an
other
presents as spiritual,
the amazing capacity to
give and feel love
even if
for the briefest
of moments.

- barakah | blessing

beneath it
aching
in the softness of me
where longing builds her home
is where i miss you.

- how the anger saves me

i believed we were standing at her
salt-water breast
looked back
discovered
an aquarium of stale water,
floating carcasses.

- hindsight, that 20/20

*but*
*what if i wake*
*to find the weight of us*
*through conjured hands*
*has fractured my larynx?*
he asks.

there are some
who when trusted (by our softness)
feel a shackle (of their resentment)
fasten around their throat.

*the weight of us*
*has bruised my neck*
he continues.

and my neck, i think
its soft curve
the flavour of which you would not have tasted
in months.

what else can they do
but break it?

- fear of commitment | the unfaithful

snare,
he bent himself
around me;
we,
frozen in amber
our fit, perfect.

i wake
to shards of amber in wet eyes,
dust in my throat.

i am no longer there,
every woman
a substitute.

- jigsaw

we exist

pieces unmatched, awkward angles,
drawn
inside an etch a sketch.

she picks it up
and shakes shake shake

we are non-existent.

- the new girlfriend

preferring instead to open my breast to rage
shallow
unkind and biting hate
until

i saw her face
soft, porcelain skin
protecting breakable features
finest bone China
sorrow-full eyes drowning in themselves
bewildered
asking *why was i not loved?*

sorrow-full eyes
just as mine had been
asking *why was i not loved?*
just as i had been.

- tea with the new woman he left for another

do you like it?
it's stiff. feels strange. smells off. what is it? i ask
and back away.

it is all of the women i suffocated when i could not breathe.
it is all of the women i stabbed when i needed stitching.
it is all of the women i held down when i could not stand.

it is Women
because i do not know how to love my Self.

- sister, lost

silk-worm,
spin only love as cocoon
to keep your softness.

- transformation (back to self)

strength.
it should not be mistaken
for invulnerability from hurt.

- how to keep the softness iii

that i still look for you
beneath the hooded eyes
thick lashes
of strange men.

- secrets iii

watch out.

for those
offering candy hearts
on their tongues.

for those
whose measure
is by number of bodies
devoured.

for those
whose religion
is heresy against you.

for those
whose hatred
is a mask of propriety.

for those
who make an obstacle course
of your needs.

for those
whose tongues are dressed
in the finest silks.

- (fore)warning(s)

*your mouth*
*it is what men dream of*
*when next to their wives*
he tried.

moving from woman to woman like a disease,
the light at the end of the tunnel
is obstructed by pelts.

women flayed
he cannot tell the difference
between the parts he kissed
and those he sliced.

- once a hunter, always a hunter

for you to know
inside of your own skin
that you mistreated. hurt. wounded.
it is not enough.

for you to say
*i know i fucked up*
is absolutely. not under any circumstance. or measure of
integrity,
sufficient.

your self-immolation
it does not count
is not acceptable
will remain inadequate
unless it is performed
flames at your feet
standing still
before us
against whom
you threw the first match.

- the (missing) apology

to forgive

means to forgive a remembering. and the remembering
it hardens. hates. breaks. poisons. but mostly.
the remembering re-wounds. re-shapes the first breaking and
all-after breakings.

and i am so tired.

too tired to remember.

too bruised to walk forgiveness.

too weary of anything.
anyone.
myself included.
who is anything but soft.

- stranger to myself

expose your wounds -

pull out the sutures
parade teeth blood covered
highlight the bruise(s)
point. emphasize. shed light on
the chaos they leave behind.

free-fall into your sorrow
to take the voice of your most honest self,
be so vulnerable
that your tender and beautiful heart
forces (broken) eyes to the ground
*so emotional*
*how shameful*
*stiff upper lip*
*shares so much*
language, not of our culture.

scorched,
let it consume you
inside to out,
and when your skin
blisters
sloughs off
kiss your prayers
into an envelope
turn your charred roots to the ocean
cleansing,
she will at once place salt in wound
and pull pain from body.

wait for regeneration.

- an ashes to ashes transmutation

i rise through the chimney
to look down
out of body
once built of heaven's ware,
now wallpaper thinning
purple veins emerge
now misshapen walls
back bent over a short clock
now vines grow on rusted iron
tired and reluctant heart.

i am drunk by nostalgia
struggling to look at my faces of earlier seasons,
a life wasted
*because I did not marry*
*because I did not birth*
*because I did not build a home for a man*
my mother, opposite,
pride full
she shows photos of her younger self.

once citadel around my forming body
suddenly polar,
but soon
we will both be ash
no rising through chimneys
both be nothing
*how long will she wait for me*
*to go Home.*

- passing seasons

when eyes

move over you like
rose-water syrup;
no snags
no catches
smooth as a sunset-heart into the ocean,
you know
you have arrived.

- homecoming

beauty
is in the heart of the beholder.

- rewriting a terrible proverb

woman
in
love
defies.

- WILD

## ACKNOWLEDGMENTS

With all of the love and adoration I am able to give my family for their unyielding support, even when they don't understand. More still, when they are made uncomfortable by what I might write but behind me still they are always to be found. Thank you; I love you.

To Fatima Habil for lending me her own voice, to ensure that mine is sharper still. This collection is made richer by you. Maaren, she will always be in this heart.

To Destine Lord for lending me her ears, and always providing a soft spot for this sometimes weary heart. I am no longer imagining murder scenes in my head because of you. Thank you.

And last, but never the least - to my family in Occupied Gaza. We are with you. We are *always* with you.

*(Thank you to all men of ago; because of you, I am led to him.)*

**ABOUT THE AUTHOR**

Maha Zimmo was born in Benghazi, Libya, was graduated from Carleton University, where she received her Master of Arts in International Legal Theory.

Maha is a former political analyst for several online journals including rabble, has been writing for 16+ years at onefemalecanuck(dot)com, and is currently the resident advice columnist at Chai Latte Diaries, as well as a regular contributor at *sister-hood magazine*. Her poetry has been featured in ARC Poetry Magazine, Cosmonauts Avenue, METATRON Press, Across the Margin, Ottawater Poetry Journal, Taj Mahal Review, and Rise Up Review.

*the incense(d) heart* is Maha's second collection of poetry, serving as follow-up to the 2019 publication of her first book titled *rose-water syrup*.